RHYMING RAINS ON DANCING DAYS

A collection of wanderer's poems

MUDAVATH PRIYATHAM NAIK

BookLeaf Publishing

India | USA | UK

Dedication

This collection of poems is dedicated to my Dad—the man who, with only a modest education, made the most of every opportunity and still crafts beautiful lines in Telugu. He's the man who bore the weight of a surname, adding it to his own as imposed by circumstances; a man who has faced life's trials yet never hesitates to plant the seeds of harsh truths in his son.

Dad, you always taught me not to fear doing what I wish for, falling in love, or fighting for anything—and to stand strong, even if it means begging or battling for what the heart holds dear. I'll never forget your words: "If ever needed, I'll fight or beg for what you wish or love too, Chinna."

Thank you for sharing your own love story openly, for encouraging me to write, read, and think freely. Every step of my journey is owed to you—the steadfast pillar, the

strangest friend of my life, who is, in many
ways, unpredictable.

—Mudavath Priyatham Naik

Acknowledgement

First, my heartfelt thanks to my school principal, Mr. R. Vishwanadhan Nair, and my English teacher, Mrs. R. Vijayalakshmi Nair, for lending me their Wren and Martin grammar book when I had none. My first novel that I read, Malgudi Days by R.K. Narayan, was suggested by Mrs. Vijayalakshmi, and from then on, I never stopped reading. That single act of generosity sparked my journey into language and writing, shaping my foundation in ways that continue to impact me. Special thanks to Vijayalakshmi Ma'am for her role as the unofficial editor of this collection; her insights and support have enriched my work profoundly.

And, of course, special thanks to the special person who is the reason for the majority of these poems.

This book is as much yours as it is mine.

Preface

This collection of poems is a journey that began unexpectedly. I never thought I would find my voice in poetry or bring my thoughts to life on a page. But in the final days of my college graduation, something miraculous happened. Inspired by a special person—whose presence is felt within these pages—words began to flow, leading to a series of poems. From that moment, there was no looking back.

I wrote simply for the love of it, whether the poems turned out refined or rough, meaningful or mundane. Among these is "Alvidha," a piece born from the bittersweet emotions of my last day at IIT Kharagpur. Putting those feelings into words felt like a burden back then, but with some courage, I carried it through. Another is "I Met a Litchi," which is still my favorite, with the remaining poems reflecting the thoughts of a wanderer.

Each poem is a step on this unexpected path, supported by friends who encouraged me to keep going, who understood the value in every line, and who helped me believe in this journey. To them, and to the spark that started it all, I owe my deepest gratitude.

Rhyming Rains on Dancing Days

When all things go right,
the day stays all the way humble.
When everything goes silent,
all the days go numb.

When no one goes high,
all day it gets dumb.
When no one cares about all the cheers,
the day gets into a state of a mob.

When all the stupidity is seen by rain,
the day's interest succumbs.
The day asks itself, whether rain
rhymes based on my moments
or the other way around.
Knowing this, the day keeps reiterating,
the rains to see whether they
rhyme based on my dance!

Prisoner in Paradise

Her rage is not a barrier
For him to stop talking to the girl,
Her age is not a privilege
For him to decide that girl,
Her wages are not the thing
He gets for his own savage.
Her little crispy nose is what
He deserves from the girl.
Her fears are his only eve for sadness,
Her smile is his only source of happiness.
Her eyes drowned in her lens and tears,
Her only destiny—and the eyes make him
More a human than a prisoner in paradise!

The unknown someone

Known someone, known someone,
known them for a while.
Known someone, known someone,
until they found someone.
Known someone, known someone,
before time never freed them.
Known someone, known someone,
when nights just blinked away.
Known someone, known someone,
until losing them is the fright.
Known someone, known someone,
until the extreme comparison is made.
Known someone, known someone,
until they never spoke to.
Known someone, known someone,
until they became unknown.

I met a litchi

I met a girl
in the litchi's farm.
I met a girl
when litchis blossomed,
startled, wondered,
which litchi is best
for a feast, looked
everywhere, up till the sky.
Eyes searching for the
most shiny, spherical ones,
waiting for their best scents,
mouth for their best
taste ever to come,
heart waiting for its
most tempestuous beat,
beating for the one.
Litchi that can calm
my mind and racing heart,
searching in the void,
looked again desperately—
there it was, in front
of me, that one litchi
that made me realize

that I met a girl!

5

Striving Freedom

All you need is some air called freedom
when you're suffocated in captivity.
All you have is the state of cage enslavement
when you don't have the key called rebellion.
All you can be is an inconvenient nationalist
when you can't be an abolitionist.
All you can be is a normal person
when you can't do something special.
Freedom is entrapped, until you
strive to find the hidden one.
After all, we ain't Che Guevara,
'cause none are gonna have that aura.

Alvidha

Is this the one last good night?
No, said the undying night.
Ain't these the best moments?
No, said the reverberating memento.
Ain't these the best winds in
a while? said every blade of grass,
every chatter, every stumbled mind,
all the shivery hands only
finding their space in the
pocket full of memories uncut,
that never wanted to fade away,
with many unheard talks, with
many unconfessed avows, with all the
untouched kisses all at once, says
It ain't about the place, it's about the people!

Statue of Poverty

They said this is the statue for our weal,
they said this is the way we heal,
they said this is the symbol of our rise,
they said this is to make us wise.
Who said this is a thriving step,
where my brothers are still
burning with unaltered poverty?
Succumbed to ashes, I stand
here, where my brothers and sisters'
ashes never stop to egress.
I am made with their bones and
decorated with their thrombus.
They said they heard the statue plead, yet
they said this is the statue of our lead!
And they said this is the way we hail!

Amidst the winters

Amidst the winters,
there was a day
which reminded me
of the hottest summer,
where the thirst can't
be quenched by
just water, touch
Is no more felt
until you touch the
cheeks, which are
surfed by tears,
until you see the eyes
which has never
stopped waiting for thee,
where you can only
hear the heart thumping
at its highest beat,
mind never stopped
thinking about
how is it gonna
erase all these memories,
every void thought
said all this has to

end one day,
how long this will take
To end up good said
her insecurity,
Will I be able to
Fight all along,
said her courage
just give it a try
said her heart!

Office Rat

Piled up with bread,
woke up late as usual,
ran across the street,
hopped onto the city bus.
Looked at many eyes
that are busy on screens.
All the horns wailing,
pedestrians amidst the rains,
looked like walking for a mile,
only for a short distance.
Every belly fat ketose,
and none's anaerobic.
Got the sight of
many shorts and jeans,
none looks perfect.
Reached a building
where all the people
are up for a rat race,
to just reach the offices.
Everyone got settled
like rats in a cage.
Something felt low,
looked for a mouth

to talk, all shut, and
looked at all the eyes again
that are busy with screens!

Her Unknown Destiny

Gazing at the parallel tracks,
she reckons something in her life
that they never meet.
Quite low, perhaps, they both run,
in their parallel axes.
Only the railroad binds them.
Beneath, though, can never be seen.
She reckons her bond with someone—
a so-called bond that existed virtually,
having a glance through
a hole in the world's darkness.
Little known to her, she was
bound to those bars of
her homemade prison.
Little known to her, she cannot
make the tracks meet,
running at a low distance, parting.
A little unknown to the little one,
defining life is a void task,
to meet up with something undesired.
Is it worthwhile calling her life,
looking through the lens of
her family or society, or is it a

so-called life that remains undefined?

1000 watts

All of a sudden felt missing someone,
missed the perfume, can still smell
the bits and traces of hair strands left
only reminding of the stranded bond
hoping all this should go away one day,
still, remember the way she shines
Just like she did the 1st time
we had met, just like a 1000W bulb,
shoulders never forget the
way she lied on 'em once,
heart will never stop wandering for
the moment of being out with her
mind just getting ready for a forever
one-sided long relationship
the most ignored part soul just begs
why can't this 1000w bulb
shine on me again and why
should this happen only to me?

All the time

All the time you won't be alone,
said my sister.
All the time you won't be desperate,
said my love.
All the time you won't be careless,
said my friends.
All the time you won't be irrational,
said my teachers.
All the time you won't be happy,
said my depression.
All the time you won't be calm,
said my temperament.
In all the difficult times, I'll be with you,
said my stone heart.

Suppressed Revolution

Someone ain't opening his mouth
about the atrocities,
'cause everyone was shushed
with the complimentary
incentives. Let the insects fly,
let the roundworms roam
in the so-called eatables,
said the indolence of action.
Nothing is going to happen,
said someone who already
tried this. Let's boycott,
said the young blood.
After consequences will result
in nothing, said someone.
After all, we ain't Che Guevara
to fight for our rightful. After all,
he is a man of revolution, who just
rode his continent on La Poderosa.
The ideology doesn't matter, 'cause
someone ain't opening his mouth.

The last dance

Between the creak sounds and
shuttle noise, there lay a dance—
a dance done by many of
my peeps, a dance that we craved
for day and night, and all the time,
a dance that led to hamstrings and
all the god-known injuries,
which gave an extra thrust
to play more. Which ain't a play—
it's a dance for life,
a dance to forget all the pressure,
a dance to forget ourselves,
a dance with only racket and nets.
And then comes a day for the
last dance, where the last
creak sound went unheard, the
shuttle noise got suppressed
amidst the dance, knowing that
it'll be the last dance forever.
The racket and shuttle made
their best cracking sounds!

The Goat Departed

Festive customs are done,
a prayer was held to
the goddess who likes blood,
and the blood to give was
widespread, all over decorating
the arena with the beat red.
The goat's head was axed,
served as the sacred food.
The goat never knew it'd be
part of such a great ritual.
It never knew that its blood
would be taken as a ritualistic one.
When sunshine kissed, it had its
straws; it didn't know that it was its
last, so it greeted well with all of them,
played cheerfully, though it was
tied to the strongest tree. Yet it had
its fun and thought the people
around it were very kind. They were
too kind that they didn't allow its
blood to fall on the ground, collected,
cooked, and every last inch was
served as it was finger-licking good.

One among many pitied the goat,
yet they say the dish is too good—
taste supersedes humanity,
said someone. Why don't we eat
vegan? thought someone, 'cause
it's too good; you can't stop this.

Dating Waiting

Swiped right, swiped left,
to find no proper match.
Have given the prompts,
nothing gets exempt.
Dumped a bit of earnings
to bloom the matching chances,
increased the match radius,
only to find obscure faces,
or too thin, too fat to see.
Thought a book shouldn't
be judged by its cover,
but this ain't a book; this
is something a life bets on.
Realizing you shouldn't force
a match, that occurs naturally,
as if an earthquake occurs
without warning, devastating
the life and being. After,
these should happen one day!

6 AM

It's 6 AM,
just hopped on the train.
My eyes barely remember
my last sleep, hustled on
to my berth, jostled with
my perished hair. Set up
the bed and fell off to sleep.
Meanwhile, an old man
gazed at the tracks outside,
gave a gentle smile to me,
again smiled, indicating as if
these days teenagers are way out of life.
"6 AM is the time you'd wake,"
the kid said with his cunning smile.
Gone are those days,
when people aged like you
must be so active at this time,
said his vicious eyes.
Bedsheets were wrapped,
and the chilling temperatures
led me to doze off.
Luckily, there were no smiles further!

Rightful bribe

"Dad, every inch of this plan's flawed,"
the son exclaimed, dismayed and awed.
"Why did we feed him cash in loads,
when every penny down the road
was wasted, thrown, and left behind—
our savings spent, our future blind."
The father sighed and shook his head,
"It's custom, son, they must be fed.
You give, not get—how things go,
in ways you'll come to learn and know."
"But won't they face a proper probe,
these examiners in their silk robes?"
"They're bribed, my son," the father sighed,
his words left the young boy decried.
Demented, the child felt trapped to stay,
and dreamt of leaving far away:
"I won't live here; this isn't right,
I won't get used to this hopeless fight!"
The father's voice grew soft and keen,
"We bear this all, each loss unseen.
An heir to this motherland, for better or ill—
to leave would feel like breaking will."
"So be an inconvenient nationalist,

or an insane, lost idealist or naxalist."

24

The silence

All I want is the silence from the one I love,
All I want is to keep her calm and still,
All I want is her happiness, leaving me to win,
All I want is her reflection on ourselves,
All I want is her smile to brighten up my
world,
All I want is for her success to build the
so-called steps of her career.
All I want is to fly away, fly away
until I see my star fade away.
All I want is to hop again and hop again
until I get a sigh of hope once more.
All I want is to swing high
until I reach the destination across.
All I want is to see the edge of tomorrow,
All I want is the silence from the one I love.

The violinist

The violin was tucked in,
the music taking
a whirl in all hearts.
All the notes are on a high,
the closed eyes riveting
only on the vocal sounds,
after the fiddle was
out of the neck gap.
Another violinist
started singing—
"If it was yours,
it might return to you.
If you break something,
consider it yours.
Can't the broken one
return to us?"
Leaving everyone awestruck,
the fiddle was again tucked in,
and all the people got stuck in
the violinist's grace and music.
No one knew when the song had
ended, because it ended unknowingly,
as if no one wanted to end it!

Not all those who wander are lost

Not all who wander lose their way,
Though doubts may cloud and dreams may
sway.
For in each pause, a spark may start,
To guide the mind, to stir the heart.
The world can tempt with paths askew,
When goals feel faint and hard to view.
Yet sometimes aimless steps prepare
For journeys bold and futures rare.
We've seen the lost, the dreamers roam,
Their hearts adrift, far from their home.
But purpose calls when needs arise,
To shape the course, to clear the skies.
So let us wander, yet beware—
Our dreams need roots, and a purpose there.
For though we stray, our hearts can see
The path that leads to destiny.